How Sweet the Sound

Amazing Grace...
How Sweet The Sound

D. Morgan®

HARVEST HOUSE PUBLISHERS
EUGENE, OREGON 97402

How Sweet the Sound

Text Copyright © 2001 by Harvest House Publishers
Eugene, Oregon 97402

ISBN 0-7369-0576-6

Artwork designs are reproduced under license from © Arts Uniq' ®, Inc., Cookeville,
TN and may not be reproduced without permission. For more information regarding
art prints featured in this book, please contact:

Arts Uniq'
P.O. Box 3085
Cookeville, TN 38502
1.800.223.5020

Design and production by Koechel Peterson and Associates, Minneapolis, Minnesota

Unless otherwise indicated, Scripture quotations are taken from the Holy Bible,
New International Version®, Copyright © 1973, 1978, 1984 by the International
Bible Society. Used by permission of Zondervan Publishing House. Scripture quotations
marked KJV are from the King James Version.

Harvest House Publishers has made every effort to trace the ownership of all poems
and quotes. In the event of a question arising from the use of a poem or quote, we
regret any error made and will be pleased to make the necessary correction in future
editions of this book.

Manufactured in China.

01 02 03 04 05 06 07 08 09 10 / IM /10 9 8 7 6 5 4 3 2 1

Seated one day at the organ,
I was weary and ill at ease,
And my fingers wandered idly
Over the noisy keys.
I do not know what I was playing,
Or what I was dreaming then,
But I struck one chord of music
Like the sound of a great Amen.

ADELAIDE A. PROCTOR

In His love,
I am free...

Rock of Ages

D. Morgan © 2001   ...Rock of Ages
Cleft for me.

Rock of Ages

Rock of Ages, cleft for me,

Let me hide myself in Thee;

Let the water and the blood,

From Thy wounded side which flowed,

Be of sin the double cure,

Save from wrath and make me pure.

Trust in the Lord forever, for the Lord, the Lord, is the Rock eternal.

ISAIAH 26:4

THE ORIGINAL TITLE OF THIS HYMN WAS "A LIVING AND DYING PRAYER FOR THE HOLIEST BELIEVER IN THE WORLD." AUGUSTUS TOPLADY PENNED THIS FAMOUS HYMN IN 1775 TO EXPRESS HIS GRATITUDE FOR THE UNBELIEVABLE GRACE AND FORGIVENESS THAT THE LORD GIVES TO THOSE WHO TRUST IN HIM.

God will pardon me: that's His business.

HEINRICH HEINE

The Lord is my Rock, my fortress and my deliverer; my God is my Rock, in whom I take refuge.

PSALM 18:2

If the basis of peace is God, the secret of peace is trust.

JOHN BENJAMIN FIGGIS

The high that proved too high,
the heroic for earth too hard,
The passion that left the ground
to lose itself in the sky,
Are music sent up to God
by the lover and the bard;
Enough that he heard it once;
we shall hear it by-and-by.

ROBERT BROWNING

Of all the earthly music, that which reaches farthest
into heaven is the beating of a truly loving heart.

HENRY WARD BEECHER

D. Morgan

Found again
Sweet memories
Of childhood

...The
Church
In
The Wildwood.

Round the bend...

D. Morgan © 2001

The Church in the Wildwood

There's a church in the valley by the wildwood,

No lovelier spot in the dale;

No place is so dear to my childhood,

As the little brown church in the vale.

I love thy Church, O God!
Her walls before Thee stand,
Dear as the apple of Thine eye,
And graven in Thy hand.

TIMOTHY DWIGHT

THIS BELOVED HYMN OF THE MIDWEST WAS WRITTEN BY DR. WILLIAM
PITTS IN 1857 ON HIS WAY TO SEE HIS BRIDE-TO-BE. HE WAS SO INSPIRED
BY THE BEAUTY OF THE SPOT HE STOPPED TO REST IN THAT HE FELT THE
NEED TO WRITE IT DOWN IN VERSE FORM AND SET IT TO MUSIC.

Surely goodness and love
will follow me all
the days of my life,
and I will dwell
in the house of
the Lord forever.

PSALM 23:6

A house of comfort...
where hope is given;
A source of strength...
to make earth heaven.
A shrine of worship...
a place to pray—
I found all this...
in my church today.

CYRUS E. ALBERTSON

On this rock I will
build my church, and
the gates of Hades
will not overcome it.

MATTHEW 16:18

The best and most beautiful things
in the world cannot be seen or even touched.
They must be felt with the heart.

HELEN KELLER

The body is truly the garment of the soul,
which has a living voice;
for that reason it is fitting that the body,
simultaneously with the soul,
repeatedly sings praises to God through the voice.

HILDEGARD VON BINGEN

A babe of humble birth
Became the greatest King...

...Joy To The World

Let heaven and nature sing.

Joy to the World

D. Morgan ©2001

Joy to the World

He rules the world with truth and grace,

And makes the nations prove

The glories of His righteousness

And wonders of His love.

"Today in the town of David a Savior has been born to you; he is Christ the Lord. This will be a sign to you: You will find a baby wrapped in cloths and lying in a manger." Suddenly a great company of the heavenly host appeared with the angel, praising God and saying, "Glory to God in the highest, and on earth peace to men on whom his favor rests."

LUKE 2:11-14

THIS CHRISTMAS CLASSIC COMES FROM ISAAC WATT'S 1719 COLLECTION OF HYMNS IN WHICH HE ATTEMPTED TO PUT MOST OF THE 150 PSALMS INTO PARAPHRASED LYRICS. WITH THIS SONG, HE WANTED TO EXPRESS HIS PRAISE FOR THE GIFT OF SALVATION THROUGH THE BABE BORN IN BETHLEHEM.

If there is joy in the world, surely the man of pure heart possesses it.

THOMAS À KEMPIS

Shout for joy to the Lord, all the earth, burst into jubilant song with music.

PSALM 98:4

Joy is the serious business of heaven.

C. S. LEWIS

Do all the good you can,
by all the means you can,
in all the ways you can,
in all the places you can,
at all the times you can,
to all the people you can,
as long as ever you can.

JOHN WESLEY

Come then, expressive silence, muse His praise.

JAMES THOMSON

The prophecy kept
The promise fulfilled...

...Faith of Our Fathers
Living Still.

D. Morgan © 2001

Faith of Our Fathers

Faith of our fathers! We will strive

To win all nations unto thee,

And through the truth that comes from God

Mankind shall then be truly free:

Faith of our fathers, holy faith!

We will be true to thee til death.

*Now faith is being sure
of what we hope for and
certain of what we do not see.
This is what the ancients
were commended for.*

HEBREWS 11:1-2

*God didn't call us
to be successful,
just faithful.*

MOTHER TERESA

*Faith is our spiritual oxygen.
It not only keeps us alive in God,
but enables us to grow stronger...*

JOYCE LANDORF HEATHERLEY

*Some faced jeers and flogging,
while still others were
chained and put in prison.
They were stoned;
they were sawed in two;
they were put to death
by the sword...the world
was not worthy of them...
These were all commended
for their faith...*

HEBREWS 11:36-39

THIS HYMN WAS WRITTEN IN 1849 BY FREDERICK FABER AS A TRIBUTE TO THOSE WHO WERE PERSECUTED FOR UPHOLDING THE FAITH. HE WANTED A SONG TO REFLECT HIS GRATITUDE FOR ALL THE MARTYRS WHO HAD COME BEFORE HIM AND GIVEN THEIR LIVES TO PROCLAIM THE MESSAGE OF CHRIST.

The song
Of summer
Sings
Again...

D. Morgan® 2000

...The old
Sweet
Story.

Our strength often increases in proportion
to the obstacles imposed upon it.

PAUL DE RAPIN

Seeing our Father in everything
makes life one long thanksgiving
and gives rest of the heart.

HANNAH WHITHALL-SMITH

I love to tell the story;
'Tis pleasant to repeat
What seems each time I tell it,
More wonderfully sweet...
I love to tell the story,
'Twill be my theme in glory
To tell the old, old story
Of Jesus and His love.

KATHERINE HANKEY

A whole new world
When first I found

Amazing Grace...
...How Sweet The
Sound.

D. Morgan © 2000

Amazing Grace

Amazing Grace

Amazing grace! how sweet the sound,
That saved a wretch like me!
I once was lost, but now am found,
Was blind, but now I see.

His grace is great enough to meet the great things—
The crashing waves that overwhelm the soul,
The roaring winds that leave us stunned and breathless,
The sudden storms beyond our life's control.
His grace is great enough to meet the small things—
The little pin-prick troubles that annoy,
The insect worries, buzzing and persistent,
The squeaking wheels that grate upon our joy.

ANNIE JOHNSON FLINT

ENGLISHMAN JOHN NEWTON WROTE THIS SIMPLE HYMN AS A GIFT TO
HIS CONGREGATION THAT CONSISTED MOSTLY OF HARDWORKING,
DEDICATED LABORERS. THIS FAVORITE HYMN REFLECTS THE LIFE-CHANGING
EXPERIENCE THAT HE FELT WHEN HE SURRENDERED HIS HEART TO GOD.

Grace is the good pleasure of God
that inclines Him to bestow
benefits upon the undeserving.

A.W. TOZER

For it is by grace you have been saved,
through faith—and this not from yourselves,
it is the gift of God—not by works,
so that no one can boast.

EPHESIANS 2:8,9

The will of God will never take you
where the grace of God cannot keep you.

AUTHOR UNKNOWN

Therefore, since we have been
justified through faith, we have
peace with God through our
Lord Jesus Christ, through whom
we have gained access by faith
into this grace in which
we now stand. And we rejoice
in the hope of the glory of God.

ROMANS 5:1,2

Grace is but glory begun,
and glory is but grace perfected.

JONATHAN EDWARDS

Thus all below is strength,
and all above is grace.

JOHN DRYDEN

God writes with a pen
that never blots,
speaks with a tongue
that never slips,
and acts with a hand
that never fails.

AUTHOR UNKNOWN

Where words fail, music speaks.

HANS CHRISTIAN ANDERSEN

The music plays
The heart remembers...
...And the
Melody
Lingers
On.

D. Morgan

There...is a stirring
Within my heart

Each time I remember...
How Great Thou Art.

How Great Thou Art

D. Morgan® ©2000

How Great Thou Art

What unnumbered cathedrals has

He reared in the forest shades,

vast and grand, full of curious carvings,

and haunted evermore by tremulous music;

and in the heavens above, how do stars

seem to have flown out of His hand faster

than sparks out of a mighty forge!

HENRY WARD BEECHER

*The heavens declare the glory of God;
the skies proclaim the work of his hands.*

PSALM 19:1

THE ORIGIN OF THIS WELL-TRAVELED HYMN BEGAN IN SWEDEN WITH A SIMPLE LAY PREACHER WHO EDITED A WEEKLY CHRISTIAN NEWSPAPER. IT SOON BECAME VERY POPULAR AMONG WORSHIPERS. A GERMAN TRANSLATION SOON APPEARED AND A RUSSIAN ONE FOLLOWED THAT. A MISSIONARY, STUART K. HINE, SAW THE TEXT IN MOSCOW AND BROUGHT IT BACK WITH HIM TO ENGLAND AFTER THE START OF WORLD WAR II. IT GAINED IMMENSE POPULARITY IN NORTH AMERICA WHEN IT WAS INTRODUCED AT A BILLY GRAHAM CRUSADE IN CANADA.

*Bless the Lord, O my soul.
O Lord my God,
thou art very great;
thou art clothed with
honour and majesty*

PSALM 104:1 (KJV)

*I never trod a rock so bare,
Unblessed by
verdure-brightened sod,
But some small flower,
half-hidden there,
Exhaled the fragrant
breath of God.*

ANONYMOUS

*He fills his hands
with lightning and commands
it to strike its mark.
His thunder announces
the coming storm;
even the cattle make
known its approach.*

JOB 36:32,33

From sweet and tender yesterdays
Our hearts find a rest
There with gentle memories
And friends who know us best.

D. Morgan © 1999

*I have always kept one end in view,
namely . . . to conduct a well-regulated
church music to the honor of God.*

JOHANN SEBASTIAN BACH

*Music hath charm
to soothe a savage breast,
To soften rocks,
or bend a knotted oak.*

WILLIAM CONGREVE

Lead me Precious Warden...

...Deep River, My home is over Jordan.

D. Morgan © 200

My Home Is Over Jordan

Deep River, my home is over Jordan, Deep River,

Lord, I want to cross over into camp ground;

Lord, I want to cross over into camp ground…

This world is but the vestibule of eternity. Every good thought or deed touches a chord that vibrates in heaven.

ANONYMOUS

THIS HISTORICALLY RICH NEGRO SPIRITUAL ORIGINATED IN GUILFORD COUNTY, NORTH CAROLINA. IT EMOTES THE FEELING THAT MANY SLAVES FELT DURING THE 1800S AND REITERATES THE LONGING TO RETURN TO THEIR HOMELAND.

There is a river whose streams make glad the city of God, the holy place where the Most High dwells.

PSALM 46:4

If God hath made this world so fair Where sin and death abound, How beautiful beyond compare Will paradise be found.

JAMES MONTGOMERY

Then the angel showed me the river of the water of life, as clear as crystal, flowing from the throne of God.

REVELATION 22:1

Music is one of the closest link-ups with God
that we can probably experience.
I think it's a common vibrating tone
of the musical notes that holds all life together.

MARVIN GAYE

O for a thousand tongues to sing
My great Redeemer's praise,
The glories of my God and King,
The triumphs of His grace!

CHARLES WESLEY

Music is an agreeable harmony for the honor
of God and the permissible delights of the soul.

JOHANN SEBASTIAN BACH

I am forever
In Your
Loving
Care...

...It's me,
Oh Lord
Standing in the need
Of Prayer

D. Morgan © 2001

Standing in the Need of Prayer

It's a me,

It's a me, O Lord,

Standin' in the need of prayer.

Not my brother,

Not my sister,

It's a me, O Lord,

Standin' in the need of prayer.

Prayer is the burden of a sigh,
The falling of a tear,
The upward glancing of an eye,
When none but God is near.

JAMES MONTGOMERY

THIS NEGRO SPIRITUAL HAS BEEN POPULAR FOR CENTURIES. IT HAS BEEN THOUGHT TO HAVE ORIGINATED IN THE SOUTH IN THE 1800s. TODAY IT IS STILL A FAVORITE AMONG CHURCHGOERS AND RECORDING ARTISTS ALIKE.

The prayer of a righteous man is powerful and effective.

JAMES 5:16

Every time you pray, if your prayer is sincere, there will be new feeling and new meaning in it which will give you fresh courage.

FYODOR DOSTOEVSKI

Therefore I tell you, whatever you ask for in prayer, believe that you have received it, and it will be yours.

MARK 11:24

Prayer is the link that connects us with God. This is the bridge that spans every gulf and bears us over every abyss of danger or of need.

A. B. SIMPSON

Hear my prayer, O Lord, listen to my cry for help.

PSALM 39:12

From the beginning
Through Eternity
I see . . .

. . . That Ol'-Time Religion,
It's good enough
For
Me.

D. Morgan ® © 2001

Ol' Time Religion

Give me that ol' time religion,

Give me that ol' time religion,

Give me that ol' time religion,

And it's good enough for me.

Teach me knowledge and good judgment,
for I believe in your commands.

PSALM 119:66

I would not give much for your religion
unless it can be seen.
Lamps do not talk, but they do shine.

CHARLES SPURGEON

THE ORIGINS OF THIS FAMILIAR GOSPEL FAVORITE ARE UNKNOWN. IT WAS FIRST
PUBLISHED BY CHARLES DAVIS TILLMAN IN 1887 AFTER HE HEARD IT BEING
SUNG BY A GROUP OF AFRICAN-AMERICANS AT A CAMP REVIVAL MEETING.

The true religion is built upon
the Rock; the rest are tossed
upon the waves of time.

SIR FRANCIS BACON

If anyone considers himself religious
and yet does not keep a tight rein on
his tongue, he deceives himself and
his religion is worthless.

JAMES 1:26

Religion brings to man an inner
strength, spiritual light, ineffable peace.

ALEXIS CARREL

Come, let us bow down in worship,
let us kneel before the Lord our Maker;
for he is our God and we
are the people of his pasture,
the flock under his care.

PSALM 95:6,7

Religion is something you do,
not something you wait for.

CHARLES G. FINNEY

That little country church
From childhood memory seems
To warm my heart as nothing can
If only in my dreams.

Music causes us to think eloquently.

RALPH WALDO EMERSON

Then at last the grandmother spoke,
"Heidi, read me one of the hymns!
I can feel I can do nothing
for the remainder of my life
but thank the Father in Heaven
for all the mercies he has shown us!"

JOHANNA SPYRI

HEIDI

I'll come back
Wherever I roam . . .

. . . Swing Low Sweet Chariot

Comin'
For to
Carry me
Home.

D. Morgan © 2001

Swing Low, Sweet Chariot

Swing low, sweet chariot,

Coming for to carry me home,

Swing low, sweet chariot,

Coming for to carry me home.

I looked over Jordan, and what did I see?

Coming for to carry me home,

A band of angels coming after me,

Coming for to carry me home.

Aim at heaven and you get earth thrown in.
Aim at earth and you get neither.

C. S. LEWIS

THIS CLASSIC SPIRITUAL IS FAVORED BY BOTH YOUNG AND OLD ALIKE. THE FIRST LINES OF THE SONG ARE ATTRIBUTED TO THE LIFE STORY OF ALEXANDER CRUMMELL WHO WAS AN AFRICAN-AMERICAN MISSIONARY TO LIBERIA IN THE 1800S. AFTER RETURNING TO THE STATES, HE LONGED TO BE BACK IN LIBERIA WITH HIS PEOPLE.

Music, the greatest good
that mortals know,
And all of heaven we have below.

JOSEPH ADDISON

The chariots of God
are tens of thousands.

PSALM 68:17

Their appearance was uncouth,
their language funny, but their hearts
were human and their singing
stirred men with a mighty power.

W.E.B. DU BOIS
The Souls of Black Folk

For he will command his
angels concerning you to guard you
in all your ways; they will lift you up
in their hands, so that you will not
strike your foot against a stone.

PSALM 91:11,12

I believe in prayer. It's the best way
we have to draw strength from heaven.

JOSEPHINE BAKER

Begin, my tongue, some heav'nly theme,
And speak some boundless thing;
The mighty works or mightier name
Of our eternal King.

Oh, might I hear Thy heav'nly tongue
But whisper, "Thou art mine!"
Those gentle words should raise my song
To notes almost divine.

ISAAC WATTS

I like the silent church before the service begins
better than any preaching.

RALPH WALDO EMERSON

Beth at last touched
the great instrument,
and straightaway
forgot her fear, herself,
and everything else
but the unspeakable delight
which the music gave her,
for it was like the voice
of a beloved friend.

LOUISA MAY ALCOTT
LITTLE WOMEN

Softly and Tenderly

The air is crisp ~
Leaves are falling
Softly and Tenderly...
...Memories Are
Calling

D. Morgan © 2000

Softly and Tenderly

Softly and tenderly, Jesus is calling,

Calling for you and for me;

See on the portals He's waiting and watching,

Watching for you and for me.

*Behold, I stand at the door,
and knock: if any man
hear my voice,
and open the door,
I will come in to him,
and will sup with him,
and he with me.*

REVELATION 3:20 (KJV)

*It is a great thing to know that if
the eternal doors swing wide open
the other way for you, you have a Friend
on the other side waiting to receive you.*

HOWARD KELLY

*We are saved by someone
doing for us what
we cannot do for ourselves.*

DONALD LESTER

*Let us therefore come boldly unto
the throne of grace, that we may
obtain mercy, and find grace
to help in time of need.*

HEBREWS 4:16 (KJV)

THIS HYMN OF INVITATION WAS WRITTEN BY WILL THOMPSON, WHO FOUND HIMSELF INSPIRED BY THE EVANGELISTIC EFFORTS OF D.L. MOODY, IRA D. SANKEY, AND OTHER PREACHERS OF THE GOSPEL DURING THE LATE 1800S. IT WAS RUMORED TO BE D. L. MOODY'S FAVORITE PIECE OF MUSIC.

Springtime in the valley
Flowers bloom with sweet perfume
And then   hearts are light,
          Spirits   bright . . .

D. Morgan© 1999

. . . The world
          Is
      New
Again .

What is a church?
Our honest sexton tells,
'Tis a tall building,
with a tower and bells.

GEORGE CRABBE

Lord, bless my church out in the wood,
For You her walls have faithful stood.
I pray that there we worship well
And reach out to those we need to tell.

VERONICA CURTIS

As real this moment
As yesterday

That Old Rugged Cross...
...On a hill far away.

D. Morgan © 2000

The Old Rugged Cross

We ourselves now know by experience that
there is no place for comfort like the cross.
It is a tree stripped of all foliage,
and apparently dead;
yet we sit under its shadow
with great delight, and its fruit
is sweet unto our taste.

CHARLES H. SPURGEON

Carry the cross patiently,
and with perfect submission;
and in the end it shall carry you.

THOMAS À KEMPIS

REVEREND GEORGE BENNARD WROTE THIS HYMN AS A PICTURE OF THE REDEMPTION
PROVIDED BY THE SAVIOR. HE FELT THAT IF HE COULD BRING JOHN 3:16 TO LIFE
THROUGH SONG, HE COULD REACH THOUSANDS WITH THE MESSAGE OF CHRIST.

For God so loved the world
that he gave his one
and only Son, that whoever
believes in him shall not perish
but have eternal life.

JOHN 3:16

The cross is the
only ladder high enough
to touch Heaven's threshold.

GEORGE DANA BOARDMAN

He forgave us all
our sins, having canceled
the written code,
with its regulations,
that was against us
and that stood opposed to us;
he took it away,
nailing it to the cross.

COLOSSIANS 2:13,14

*As the earth can produce nothing
unless it is fertilized by the sun,
so we can do nothing without the grace of God.*
VIANNEY